I0447702

Basic Guidance for Public Information Officers (PIOs)

National Incident Management System (NIMS)

FEMA 517/November 2007

FEMA

This Page Intentionally Left Blank

CONTENTS

Chapter 1: Introduction and the Incident Command System (ICS)..........................1

The Incident Command System (ICS) 1

Chapter 2: Preparedness..4

Public Education Campaigns 4

Training 4

Exercises..5

Media Relations 6

Considerations for Special Needs Populations 6

Communications Equipment and Resources 6

Joint Information System (JIS)/Joint Information Center (JIC) Planning 7

Contact Lists..8

Go Kits...8

Additional Public Information Support...8

Emergency Management Assistance Compact (EMAC) 9

Chapter 3: Disaster/Emergency Response 10

Roles of PIOs in Emergency Response...10

Informing the Public and Additional Audiences 11

Planning Considerations 13

Chapter 4: Joint Information System (JIS) and Joint Information Center (JIC)....14

Joint Information System (JIS)..14

Joint Information Center (JIC) 14

Common Roles and Functions..16

Demobilizing the Joint Information Center (JIC) 20

Chapter 5: Recovery 21

Recovery 21

Recovery Evaluation 21

Chapter 6: Integrating with Federal Support 23

Communications Protocols 24

National Incident Communications Conference Line (NICCL) 24

State Incident Communications Conference Line (SICCL).................................25

LIST OF TABLES

Table 1—PIO Major Responsibilities Checklist 10

Table 2—Types of Joint Information Centers (JICs) 16

LIST OF FIGURES

Figure 1—ICS Organizational Chart... 3

Figure 2—Sample Joint Information Center (JIC) Organizations and Functions .. 18

Figure 3—Federal ESF #15 Organizations and Functions – Field Level 24

Chapter 1: Introduction and the Incident Command System (ICS)

This guidance was developed in coordination with Federal, State, tribal, and local Public Information Officers (PIOs). The goal of this publication is to provide operational practices for performing PIO duties within the Incident Command System (ICS). It offers basic procedures to operate an effective Joint Information System (JIS).

During an incident or planned event, coordinated and timely communication is critical to effectively help the community. Effective and accurate communication can save lives and property, and helps ensure credibility and public trust.

This *Basic Guidance for Public Information Officers* provides fundamental guidance for any person or group delegated PIO responsibilities when informing the public is necessary.

The guidance also addresses actions for preparedness, incident response, Joint Information Centers (JICs), incident recovery, and Federal public information support. The guidance material is adaptable to individual jurisdictions and specific incident conditions.

The guidance outlined in this document is based on the Homeland Security Presidential Directive (HSPD) -5, the National Incident Management System (NIMS), and the National Response Framework (NRF). All of these elements are integrated with and supported through the Federal Emergency Support Function (ESF) #15 structure (see chapter 6).

THE INCIDENT COMMAND SYSTEM (ICS)

The ICS is a widely applicable management system designed to enable effective and efficient incident management by integrating facilities, equipment, personnel, procedures, and communications operating within a common organizational structure.

The Incident Commanders (ICs) structural organization builds from the top down; responsibility and performance begin with the ICS element and the IC. The IC(s) is/are responsible for the overall management of the incident. On most incidents, the command activity is carried out by a single IC. The need for a Unified Command (UC) occurs when an incident affects the statutory responsibility of more than one agency or jurisdiction. It provides guidelines to enable agencies with different legal, geographic, and functional responsibilities to coordinate, plan, and interact effectively.

Command encompasses the IC and the Command Staff. Command Staff positions may be established to assign/delegate responsibility for command activities that the IC cannot perform due to the complexity of the incident or other situational demands. These positions may include the Public Information Officer, Safety Officer, and Liaison Officer, in addition to others as required and assigned by the IC.

The PIO is responsible for communicating with the public, media, and/or coordinating with other agencies, as necessary, with incident related information requirements. The PIO is responsible for developing and releasing information about the incident to the news media, incident personnel, and other appropriate agencies and organizations. Depending on the size or complexity of the incident, a lead PIO should be assigned for each incident and may have assistants, as necessary, including supporting PIOs representing other responding agencies or jurisdictions.

The Safety Officer monitors incident operations and advises the IC/UC on all matters relating to operational safety, including the health and safety of emergency responder personnel.

The Liaison Officer is the IC/UC point of contact for representatives of other governmental agencies, non-governmental organizations (NGOs), and/or the private sector (with no jurisdiction or legal authority) to provide input on their agency's policies, resource availability, and other incident related matters.

The ICS has five major management functions: Command, Operations, Planning, Logistics, and Finance/Administration. This structure is modular and can extend to incorporate all elements necessary for the type, size, scope, and complexity of a given incident (figure 1).

The IC/UC normally assigns one or more Section Chiefs to manage the following ICS functional areas (the Section Chiefs are the General Staff):

- *Operations Section*
  The Operations Section is responsible for managing on-scene tactical operations to meet the incident objectives as established by the IC or UC.

- *Planning Section*
  The Planning Section collects, evaluates, and disseminates incident situational information to the IC/UC and incident management personnel.

- *Logistics Section*
  The Logistics Section meets all service and support needs for the incident, including ordering resources through appropriate procurement authorities from off-incident locations.

- *Finance/Administration Section*
  The Finance/Administration Section is responsible for all administrative and financial considerations surrounding an incident, including financial reimbursement to individuals, agencies, and departments.

Figure 1—ICS Organizational Chart

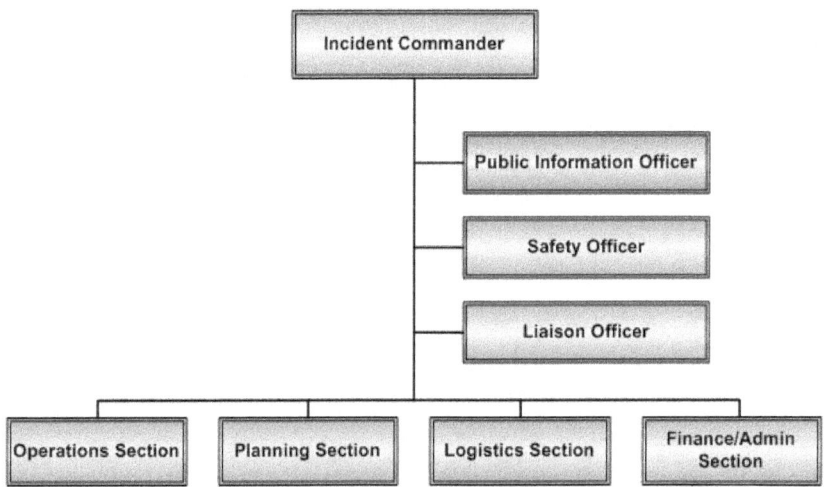

Chapter 2: Preparedness

Preparedness is essential for an effective response to an incident or planned event. Public information efforts should begin well in advance of an incident or planned event and may involve a combination of planning, resource gathering, organizing, and training and exercises. Public information planning allows for lifesaving measures such as evacuation routes, alert systems, and other public safety information, to be coordinated and communicated to diverse audiences in a timely, consistent manner. Public education contributes to preparing citizens to respond to a variety of hazards.

Public information preparedness includes developing and maintaining plans and procedures, checklists, contact lists, and public information materials. Below are some factors a PIO should consider when developing or planning prior to an incident or planned event.

PUBLIC EDUCATION CAMPAIGNS

Public education is the process of making the public aware of risks and how they can prepare for all hazards in advance.

Prior to an incident, the PIO should conduct activities to educate the public about local hazards, prevention, family preparedness, and response-level activities. It is important to develop plans and resource materials that are appropriate for a target audience such as children, special needs populations, pet owners, local governments, or entire communities.

Public education may be accomplished through events (safety fairs) or products such as media releases or packets and the distribution of brochures.

Examples of public education campaigns include:
- hurricane preparedness;
- personal preparedness and developing family or business emergency plans;
- hazardous materials awareness;
- tornado and severe weather awareness; and
- special needs population awareness.

TRAINING

PIOs should participate in ongoing training related to emergency management. This should include basic public information, ICS courses, and courses on writing media releases, conducting media interviews, and understanding the role of a JIC. Below are some of the required and recommended courses available. Additionally, public information courses are available that support NIMS through various other agencies and associations such as the Centers for Disease Control and Prevention (CDC) and the Chemical Stockpile Emergency Preparedness Program (CSEPP).

Required training for the Command and General Staff:

- Introduction to the Incident Command System (ICS-100)
  http://training.fema.gov/EMIWeb/IS/is100.asp

- ICS for Single Resources and Initial Action Incidents (ICS-200)
  http://training.fema.gov/EMIWeb/IS/is200.asp

- Intermediate Incident Command System (ICS-300)
  http://www.fema.gov/about/contact/statedr.shtm

- National Incident Management System (NIMS), An Introduction (IS-700)
  http://training.fema.gov/EMIWeb/IS/is700.asp

Recommended courses:

- Basic Public Information Officers Course (G-290)
  http://training.fema.gov/EMIWeb/EMICourses/E388.asp and
  http://www.fema.gov/about/contact/statedr.shtm

- Advanced Public Information Officer (E-388)
  http://training.fema.gov/EMIWeb/EMICourses/E388.asp

- Advanced Incident Command System (ICS-400)
  http://www.fema.gov/about/contact/statedr.shtm

- National Incident Management Systems (NIMS), Public Information Systems (IS-702)
  http://training.fema.gov/EMIWeb/IS/is702.asp

- National Response Plan (NRP), An Introduction (IS-800)
  http://training.fema.gov/EMIWeb/IS/is800a.asp

EXERCISES

Exercises provide opportunities to practice and test public information capabilities and to improve and maintain proficiency in a controlled environment. Exercises assess and validate policies, plans, and procedures, and clarify and familiarize personnel with roles and responsibilities. Exercises improve interagency coordination and communication, highlight gaps, and identify opportunities for improvement.

5

A PIO should be involved in all phases of exercises:
- planning;
- development;
- participation; and
- evaluation.

It is also recommended to involve local media in drills and exercises, and encourage them to role play during those drills and exercises in addition to covering the incident.

MEDIA RELATIONS

Working relationships with media will help during an incident. Establish a media contact list with after-business hours contact information. Keep media aware of all preparedness/awareness campaigns. Invite local media to the Emergency Operations Center (EOC), JIC, or other areas prior to any incident or planned event to show them the location and to answer questions about how information will be disseminated during an incident or planned event.

Positive media relationships built during normal day-to-day activities will be valuable during emergency situations. Do not wait until an incident to make first introductions to the media.

CONSIDERATIONS FOR SPECIAL NEEDS POPULATIONS

PIOs should be able to gather, verify, prepare, coordinate, and disseminate information to all audiences, including those with disabilities, special needs, or language requirements. It is important to have materials translated into common non-English area languages and to utilize other formats such as Braille, large print, audio, etc. Contacts should be established to translate emergency information.

Know the local media; there may be specialized newspapers or radio stations in the community that reach specific audiences. These audiences may need to be targeted during awareness/preparedness campaigns.

COMMUNICATIONS EQUIPMENT AND RESOURCES

During an incident, communication is critical to effectively help the community through the incident. Methods of communicating with the public may include the use of the Emergency Alert System (EAS), Web sites, hotlines, amateur radio, and other alerting messaging systems.

PIOs should have direct involvement in public warnings and instructions for personal safety. In major emergencies or disasters, the PIO should work closely with the warning or communications staff in issuing lifesaving or emergency information on the EAS or other means of alerting the public.

Web sites are an important tool in disseminating emergency and preparedness information. Additionally, Web sites can also be a vehicle for the media and public to submit inquiries during an incident, providing PIOs with useful information and feedback. If the agency does not have a Web site, working with local jurisdictions in order to use their Web sites for posting emergency information is recommended.

Emergency and preparedness information may include:
- press releases;
- situation reports;
- maps; and
- other emergency information.

Web logs or blogs are also important. Blogs are periodically updated journals, providing online commentary with minimal or no external editing. Media institutions have adopted this format, with many television networks, newspapers, and opinion journals now hosting blogs on their Web sites. PIOs should be aware that blogs are a part of social media reporting virtually 24/7 throughout their area of responsibility.

JOINT INFORMATION SYSTEM (JIS)/JOINT INFORMATION CENTER (JIC) PLANNING

The JIS integrates incident information and public affairs into a cohesive organization designed to provide consistent, coordinated, accurate, accessible, timely, and complete information during crisis or incident operations. The mission of the JIS is to provide a structure and system for developing and delivering coordinated interagency messages; developing, recommending, and executing public information plans and strategies on behalf of the IC; advising the IC concerning public affairs issues that could affect a response effort; and controlling rumors and inaccurate information that could undermine public confidence in the incident response effort.

The JIC is a central location that facilitates operation of the JIS. It is a location where personnel with public information responsibilities perform critical emergency information functions and crisis communications. If possible, it is advised to have location(s) identified that could be used as a JIC before an incident occurs; ideally, in close proximity to the EOC. It is important that these locations meet the working needs of the PIO function and allow easy access for the media. Once a JIC has been identified, it is recommended to have appropriate equipment and other resources available and operational. The PIO should develop standard operating procedures on the actual use of the JIC and the equipment and staff that may be needed.

CONTACT LISTS

Review and update all contact lists (e.g., media, PIO, and other agencies) every six months. Include basic information such as telephone numbers (e.g., office, home, cell), fax numbers, e-mail addresses, and Web sites.

GO KITS

It is important for the PIO to have tools and resources available for utilization during an incident. Although this is not a complete list, a Go Kit might include:
- office supplies such as pens, paper, stapler, tape, etc.;
- laptop computer and portable printer with an alternate power source(s), including accessories (e.g., memory stick, CDs, mouse, etc.);
- maps;
- television, radio, and/or broadcast recording equipment;
- cell phones/Personal Data Assistants (PDAs);
- fax machine;
- agency letterhead;
- PIO and other emergency operations plans;
- camera;
- contact lists;
- battery powered radio; and
- pre-scripted messages and template releases.

Prior to an incident or planned event, establish agreements with businesses or agencies that can assist with the operations. Examples would be contracts with: translation services; printing companies (in order to publish brochures, fact sheets, or other emergency documents); and telephone companies to install hard-line telephones.

ADDITIONAL PUBLIC INFORMATION SUPPORT

Whether the public information program consists of one person or several, it is important to develop a core group of other PIOs who can assist in the incident or planned event. These PIOs may be from other agencies or volunteers who have been trained in public information. These PIOs work at the JIC or EOC performing a variety of public information functions. Establish these relationships prior to any incident or planned event by providing EOC and JIC training, as well as other PIO training. Communicate with these PIOs on a regular basis and keep their contact information current.

EMERGENCY MANAGEMENT ASSISTANCE COMPACT (EMAC)

Another resource for PIO support is the Emergency Management Assistance Compact (EMAC). This national program that facilitates interstate mutual aid agreements could be used to provide additional public information support. For more information on EMAC, contact the State emergency management office or visit: www.emacweb.org.

Chapter 3: Disaster/Emergency Response

ROLES OF PIOS IN EMERGENCY RESPONSE

The PIO gathers, verifies, coordinates, and disseminates accurate, accessible, and timely information on the incident's cause, size, and current situation; resources committed; and other matters of general interest for both internal and external use. All information in the field must be cleared by the IC prior to release. The following table (table 1) is a sample checklist of responsibilities for the PIO in an ICS structure, which would generally apply on any incident:

Table 1—PIO Major Responsibilities Checklist

Complete	PIO Major Responsibilities
☐	Determine from the IC if there are any limits on information release.
☐	Develop material for use in media briefings.
☐	Obtain IC approval of media releases.
☐	Inform the media and conduct media briefings.
☐	Arrange for tours and other interviews or briefings, as required.
☐	Evaluate the need for and, as appropriate, establish and operate a JIS.
☐	Establish a JIC, as necessary, to coordinate and disseminate accurate and timely incident-related information.
☐	Maintain current information summaries and/or displays on the incident.
☐	Provide information on the status of the incident to assigned personnel.
☐	Maintain an Activity Log (ICS 214).
☐	Manage media and public inquiries.
☐	Coordinate emergency public information and warnings.
☐	Monitor media reporting for accuracy.
☐	Ensure that all required agency forms, reports, and documents are completed prior to demobilization.
☐	Have debriefing session with the IC prior to demobilization.

Informing the public and additional audiences during an incident is an ongoing cycle that involves four steps:

Step 1: Gather Information

Information is collected from the ICS Command and General Staff, which are a source of ongoing, official information on the response effort and other sources such as:
- response agencies;
- media;
- calls from public and elected officials;
- technical specialists;
- other agencies such as utilities and the National Weather Service; and
- emergency response guidebooks.

Step 2: Verify Information

Verify the accuracy of the information collected by consulting with:
- EOC sources and technical specialists;
- ensuring that information is consistent and accurate, striving toward accessibility to all affected by the incident; and
- other PIOs: Compare notes, especially with the lead PIO and PIOs who are liaisons to the various assistance programs or response/recovery partners, to verify the accuracy of information.

Step 3: Coordination of Information (Internal)

Coordination includes, but is not limited to:
- coordinating between ICS Command and General Staff;
- coordinating between EOC participants; and
- obtaining approval from appropriate authorities before information is disseminated.

Messaging

Initial information should include:
- actions the public should take;
- impact of the incident;
- actions the response agencies are taking;
- actions businesses and industries should take;
- a summary of the incident; and

11

- overall steps to be taken by the government and by citizens to return to normal after the incident.

Information Sharing

In addition to the public and media, information needs to be shared with the Command Staff; response community; other Federal, State, tribal, local, and volunteer agencies; elected and appointed officials, other community leaders; and other PIOs. Sharing information regarding response and recovery actions and objectives is critical to building situational awareness for a JIS.

Step 4: Dissemination of Information (External)

Information should be disseminated to:
- disaster victims;
- outside general public;
- affected jurisdictions;
- community leaders;
- private sector;
- media;
- nongovernmental organizations (NGOs) (e.g., American Red Cross);
- response and recovery organizations (e.g., urban search and rescue, utilities);
- volunteer groups (e.g., Community Emergency Response Team – CERT, Voluntary Organizations Active in Disasters – VOAD); and
- other impacted groups.

Methods of Dissemination

Dissemination may be done through multiple media outlets or alternatives, including:
- news releases;
- blogs;
- mass e-mails and faxes;
- text messages;
- Web site posting;
- EAS;
- Public Service Announcements;
- closed circuit cable;
- reverse 911;
- reader boards;
- loud speakers;
- door-to-door;
- fliers/factsheets;
- briefings; and
- community meetings.

Monitoring the Media

Verify that the public and officials are getting accurate and complete information through the media in a timely manner. Inaccuracies and rumors that affect health and safety should be addressed immediately with the media and correct information distributed through the media or other means.

PLANNING CONSIDERATIONS

The following are factors to consider in the planning of PIO operations:
- field operations (e.g., EOC, JIC);
- communications tools (e.g., cell phone, PDAs, radio);
- tasking (e.g., gathering resources such as media contacts; preparing for media conferences; creating media packets, fact sheets, background information);
- duration of operations (e.g., lodging, food, 24/7 operations);
- resource management for various locations;
- documentation (e.g., logs, time cards, media interviews);
- logistics (e.g., equipment location, supplies, power, parking, credentials); and
- evaluate staffing needs for each operational period.

Chapter 4: Joint Information System (JIS) and Joint Information Center (JIC)

JOINT INFORMATION SYSTEM (JIS)

The JIS provides the mechanism to organize, integrate, and coordinate information to ensure timely, accurate, accessible, and consistent messaging across multiple jurisdictions and/or disciplines, including the private sector and NGOs. It includes the plans, protocols, procedures, and structures used to provide information to:
- general public;
- disaster victims;
- affected jurisdictions;
- elected officials;
- community leaders;
- private sector;
- media;
- NGOs (e.g., American Red Cross);
- response and recovery organizations (e.g., urban search and rescue, utilities);
- volunteer groups (e.g., CERT, VOAD);
- international interests (e.g., international media and donations); and
- other impacted groups.

Federal, State, tribal, local, and voluntary agencies, private sector PIOs, and established JICs are critical supporting elements of the JIS. Key elements include the following:
- gathering, verifying, coordinating, and disseminating consistent messages;
- interagency coordination and integration;
- support for decision-makers; and
- flexibility, modularity, and adaptability.

Agencies issue their own releases related to their policies, procedures, programs, and capabilities; however, messages need to be coordinated utilizing the JIS to ensure message consistency.

JOINT INFORMATION CENTER (JIC)

To ensure coordination of public information during incidents that involve multiple agencies and/or jurisdictions, the IC/UC may use a JIC to support the gathering, verification, coordination, and dissemination of accurate, accessible, and timely information. The JIC is a central location that facilitates operation of the JIS. In the early stages of response to an incident, the PIO shall consult with the IC/UC regarding

14

the opening of a JIC. The IC/UC shall retain authority to order the opening of a JIC, although the lead PIO may recommend when it is appropriate.

JICs are established:
- at the direction of the IC/UC at various levels of government;
- at pre-determined or incident-specific sites; and
- as components of Federal, State, tribal, or local Multiagency Coordination Systems (MACS).

JICs may be staffed:
- by representatives from all agencies and jurisdictions involved in the response and recovery operation; and
- through intrastate and interstate mutual aid agreements such as EMAC. EMAC could be a supplemental source or vehicle for bringing trained personnel together to support a JIC.

The JIC should be located close to the best sources of information, such as an EOC, without compromising safety or security of the personnel staffing the facility. A single JIC location is preferable, but the system is flexible and adaptable enough to accommodate virtual or multiple JIC locations, as required. The following table (table 2) provides a description of different types of JICs:

Table 2—Types of Joint Information Centers (JICs)

Incident	Typically, an incident specific JIC is established at a single, on scene location in coordination with Federal, State, tribal, and local agencies or at the national level, if the situation warrants. It provides easy media access, which is paramount to success. This is a typical JIC.
Virtual	A virtual JIC is established when a physical co-location is not feasible. It connects PIOs through e-mail, cell/land-line phones, faxes, video teleconferencing, web-based information systems, etc. For a pandemic incident where PIOs at different locations communicate and coordinate public information electronically, it may be appropriate to establish a virtual JIC.
Satellite	A satellite JIC is smaller in scale than other JICs. It is established primarily to support the incident JIC and to operate under their direction. These are subordinate JICs, which are typically located closer to the scene.
Area	An area JIC supports multiple-incident ICS structures that are spread over a wide geographic area. It is typically located near the largest media market and can be established on a local, State, or multi-state basis. Multiple States experiencing storm damage may participate in an area JIC.
Support	A support JIC is established to supplement the efforts of several Incident JICs in multiple States. It offers additional staff and resources outside of the disaster area.
National	A national JIC is established when an incident requires Federal coordination and is expected to be of long duration (weeks or months) or when the incident affects a large area of the country. A national JIC is staffed by numerous Federal departments and/or agencies.

COMMON ROLES AND FUNCTIONS

The following roles and functions are common components of a JIC.

Lead PIO:
- responsible for managing the JIC;
- serves as advisor to IC/UC;
- provides overall communication policy direction;
- recommends and develops strategy for messages, briefings, and news releases;
- obtains approval from those in authority before releases are made; and
- conducts JIS/JIC briefings (live or virtual) to update staff regarding Incident Command activities.

Information Gathering:
- Response Partners – Coordination with supporting response agencies and their PIOs at EOCs, incident command posts, and other locations to gather information on the incident.
- Media Monitoring Analysis/Rapid Response – Entails reviewing media reports for accuracy, content, and possible response.
- Research and Writing:
  - Products – Writing materials such as media releases, fact sheets, flyers, etc.
  - Graphics Support – Entails designing layouts, developing PowerPoint presentations, and creating graphics for a range of materials (e.g., newsletters, flyers, etc.).
- Audio-Visual:
  - Broadcast Operations – Entails developing video documentation, special productions, remote live interview feeds, and logistical support of public meetings and presentations.
  - Photo Video – Entails providing still photography documentation to support print and internet media needs, and video documentation to support broadcast media needs. Also includes collecting materials for agency archives.

Information Dissemination:
- Briefing/Special Events – Entails handling events such as news conferences, media briefings, VIP visits, and tours for senior officials of affected areas.
- Media Relations:
  - News Desk – Serves as the primary point of contact for the media.
  - Spokesperson – Prepares and conducts regular news briefings and conferences.
- Web Support – Entails creating and maintaining web pages and blogs containing information about the incident for use by the public and the media.
- Public Inquiries – Entails responding to questions from citizens, making referrals, and developing a log of telephone calls, e-mails, etc., containing names, addresses, the type of calls, and any necessary follow up actions.

Operations Support:
- Special Needs/Multilingual – Entails providing language translation and other services to ensure appropriate and timely information reaches those in the affected areas with special needs.
- Facility Support – Coordinates with the JIC Facility Liaison to maintain and support the JIC operations concerning the facility and resources.

Liaison:
Provides a coordinated two-way communication link with key program areas and other entities involved in the response and recovery operation (e.g., elected officials, community leaders, VIPs, and other governmental and NGO support agencies).

The following diagrams (figure 2) are examples of what JIC organizations look like at various stages of an escalating incident. They are scalable and flexible; certain functions may not be needed for every type of incident or planned event. Each box represents a function to be performed. One person may do many functions, or one function may be staffed by many people, depending upon the scope of the incident.

Figure 2—Sample Joint Information Center (JIC) Organizations and Functions

Initial Response or Local Incidents

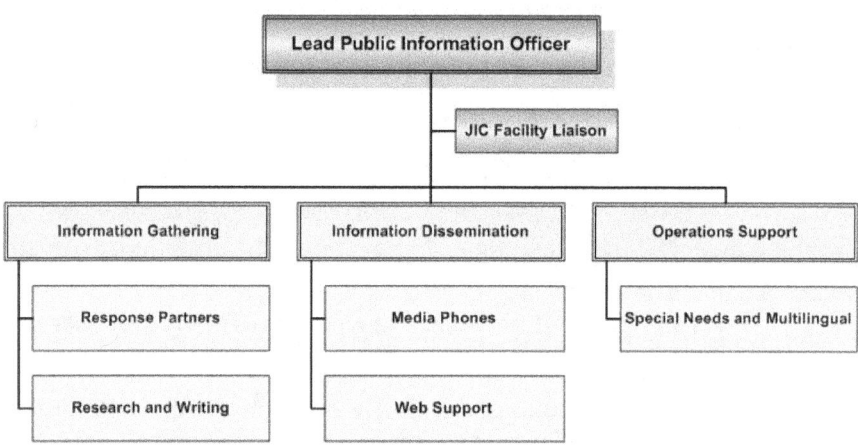

Escalating Incidents

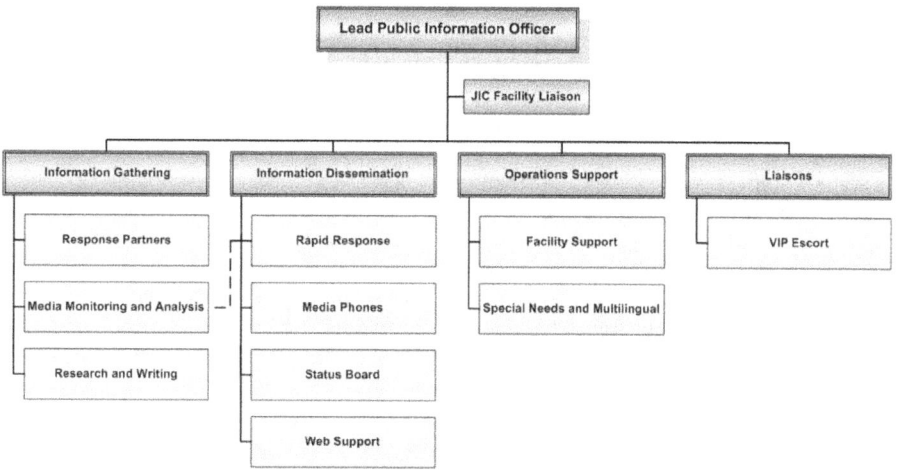

Large-Scale Incidents

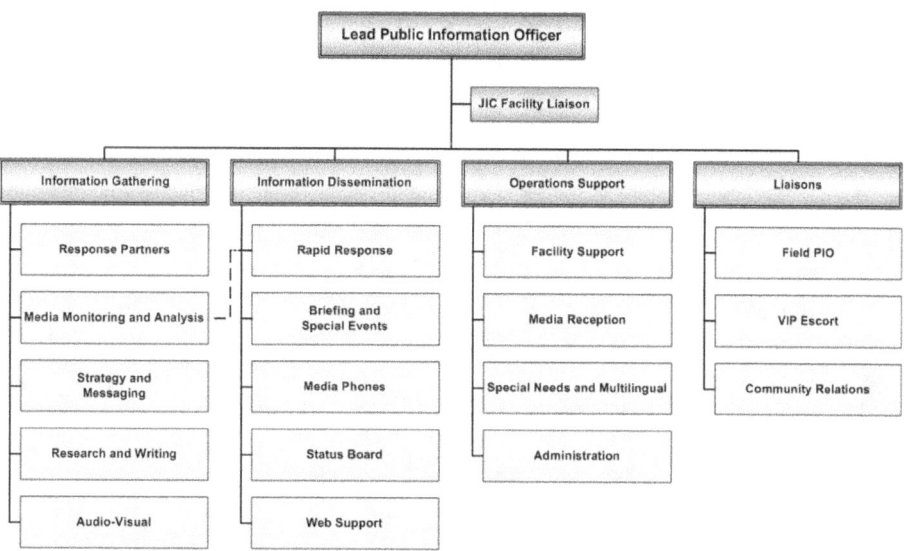

19

DEMOBILIZING THE JOINT INFORMATION CENTER (JIC)

When operational activities begin to decline, public information functions will be transferred back to responsible jurisdictions and agencies. The decision to transition will be made by the IC/UC in consultation with the lead PIO and other Section Chiefs. Below are the major steps the PIO would take in deactivating a JIC:

- prepare a comprehensive deactivation news release for lead-agency headquarters approval and distribution;
- notify community, media, agency communications managers and local officials about closing and provide regional contact information;
- provide casebooks to communication managers whose organizations will assume responsibility for ongoing information;
- complete an after-action report and participate in evaluation discussions;
- return borrowed equipment and supplies;
- inventory equipment and supplies; and
- replenish "Go Kits" as necessary.

Chapter 5: Recovery

The responsive dissemination of public information plays a critical role in the recovery process, and it begins the moment a crisis occurs. Regular communication about recovery efforts, even though response efforts may not be over, reassures the public that government agencies are working together to resolve the situation and to bring assistance to those who need it.

Communications among PIOs and the impacted audience should occur as often as necessary and continue until recovery is complete. This coordination may be accomplished through the JIC (which may still be active during the recovery phase). This information should be updated regularly and may include the following:
- actions the public should take;
- a summary of the incident or planned event;
- the impact of the incident or planned event;
- actions the response agencies are taking;
- actions the public, businesses, and industries may take to gain access to recovery programs and information on how these programs work;
- information on how to repair or restore damaged property;
- debris removal information;
- overall steps to be taken by the government and citizens to return to normal; and
- any other crisis-specific recovery information.

PIOs should:
- emphasize, as soon as appropriate, when the danger has passed or the situation has transitioned from response to recovery;
- be prepared to direct questions concerning volunteers and financial contributions to the appropriate organizations;
- inform local businesses about special programs designed to assist them through the news media, appropriate business channels, and community outreach efforts;
- communicate information on service animals, pets, and livestock; and
- coordinate with their PIO counterparts at appropriate agencies concerning environmental, ecological, and agricultural impacts.

RECOVERY EVALUATION

To help determine the effectiveness of recovery communication during an incident or planned event, PIOs should closely monitor media reports and assess public inquiries to determine if information is received and understood by its intended audiences.

Following an incident or planned event, PIOs should create a comprehensive report of media coverage, media inquiries, and public inquiries to determine the effectiveness of the recovery communications efforts. This report, or conclusions of the report, can be forwarded to the ICS planning section for inclusion in the After Action Report (AAR). The PIO should also participate in AAR reviews.

Typically, AARs contain the following components:
- Executive Summary;
- Incident Overview;
- Analysis of Capabilities;
- Major Strengths;
- Areas of Improvement; and
- Lessons Learned.

Chapter 6: Integrating with Federal Support

Federal support in an incident will operate under the standard operating procedures of Emergency Support Function (ESF) #15. Under the title of External Affairs, ESF #15 integrates and coordinates the functional areas of public affairs, community relations, State, tribal, local, and territorial affairs, the private sector, and congressional affairs. ESF #15 is led primarily by staff from the U.S. Department of Homeland Security (DHS)/Federal Emergency Management Agency (FEMA), but may also be led by personnel from other Federal agencies during specific response scenarios.

During an incident or planned event that requires a coordinated Federal response, DHS/FEMA will contact the affected State, tribal, or local jurisdictions to identify their public information needs. Based on this information, DHS/FEMA and ESF #15 will support State, tribal, and local communications plans with staff and other resources, which may include:

- satellite trucks;
- communications equipment;
- items for a media center such as TVs, computers, podiums, microphones, etc.; and
- personnel.

DHS/FEMA encourages Federal, State, tribal, and local entities to work in partnership to ensure effective and efficient emergency information is produced and disseminated. The Department encourages co-locating with the incident JIC, as it facilitates coordination, cooperation, and unified messaging between the Federal government's ESF #15 functions and their counterparts with State, tribal, and local agencies.

The following diagram shows the ESF #15 organizations and functions at the field level (figure 3). Each of the six divisions that make up ESF #15 are represented by their own organizational chart; the structure for the JIC and Planning and Products sections are shown, but they are all a part of one large organizational chart that makes up ESF #15. Each division resides in the Joint Field Office (JFO), but the JIC could co-locate with a State-operated JIC if it is not part of the JFO.

Figure 3—Federal ESF #15 Organizations and Functions – Field Level

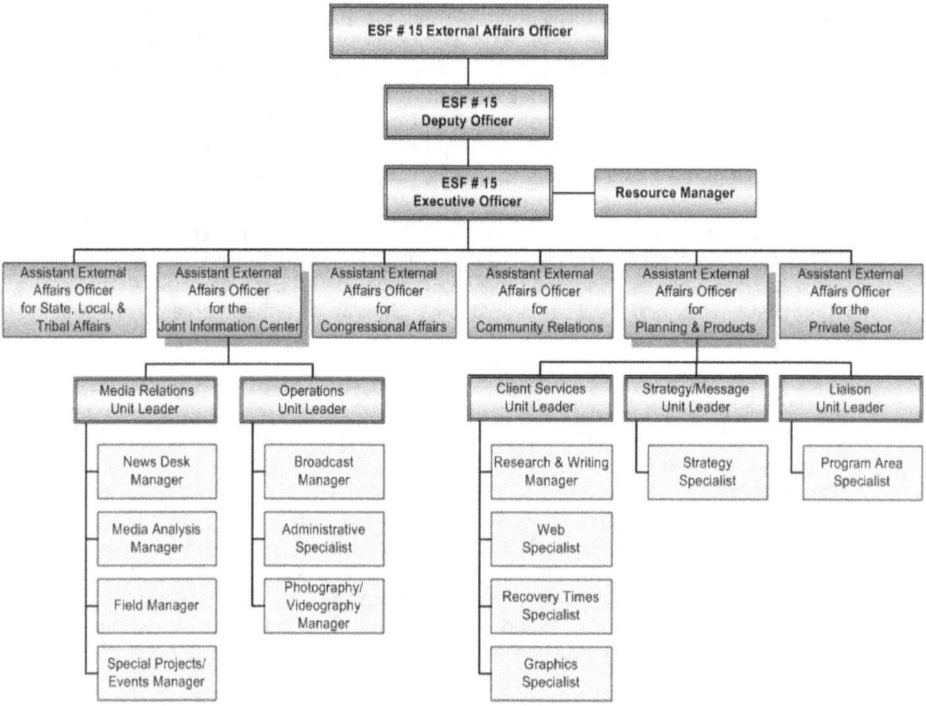

```
                    ┌──────────────────────────────────────┐
                    │ ESF # 15 External Affairs Officer     │
                    └──────────────────┬───────────────────┘
                              ┌─────────┴─────────┐
                              │ ESF # 15          │
                              │ Deputy Officer    │
                              └─────────┬─────────┘
                        ┌───────────────┴──────┐        ┌──────────────────┐
                        │ ESF # 15             ├────────┤ Resource Manager │
                        │ Executive Officer    │        └──────────────────┘
                        └───────────────┬──────┘
```

| Assistant External Affairs Officer for State, Local, & Tribal Affairs | Assistant External Affairs Officer for the Joint Information Center | Assistant External Affairs Officer for Congressional Affairs | Assistant External Affairs Officer for Community Relations | Assistant External Affairs Officer for Planning & Products | Assistant External Affairs Officer for the Private Sector |

Media Relations Unit Leader	Operations Unit Leader	Client Services Unit Leader	Strategy/Message Unit Leader	Liaison Unit Leader
News Desk Manager	Broadcast Manager	Research & Writing Manager	Strategy Specialist	Program Area Specialist
Media Analysis Manager	Administrative Specialist	Web Specialist		
Field Manager	Photography/ Videography Manager	Recovery Times Specialist		
Special Projects/ Events Manager		Graphics Specialist		

COMMUNICATIONS PROTOCOLS

Pre-identified incident communications protocols are established and ready for use during large scale incidents and incidents requiring a coordinated Federal response. Two primary tools are described below.

NATIONAL INCIDENT COMMUNICATIONS CONFERENCE LINE (NICCL)

The NICCL was created to be a single source of coordination for DHS with all other Federal agencies. It can work as a call-in conference or as an open line that can be monitored 24 hours a day for the exchange of information and updates. It is primarily for Federal-to-Federal information sharing but can also include communicators from the primarily impacted State and local community. Specifically, the NICCL:

- is used for transmission and exchange of information primarily targeted to support senior State and local officials;

- originates with DHS Public Affairs and is an executive call to discuss happening events and their agencies' roles, activities, and response; and
- is typically conducted twice daily, but it could be staffed 24 hours a day and used as an open line for information dissemination if required by an incident.

STATE INCIDENT COMMUNICATIONS CONFERENCE LINE (SICCL)

The SICCL was created primarily to bring States together to share information and discuss issues that have an effect on all of them following an incident. This line is typically used during a multiple State disaster such as a hurricane where impacted States may request support from other States. The SICCL is not a 24/7 line. Instead, it is a scheduled conference call, which would be set up as needed to address issues. In summary, the SICCL is:

- used for the transmission and exchange of information primarily targeted to State and local communicators; and
- typically activated with a multiple State incident, and there is need for cross border coordination.